ISBN 978-0-331-33535-4
PIBN 11090351

The Philadelphia Conservatory of Music

Founded in 1877

216 South Twentieth Street   *Philadelphia, Penna.*

Mrs. D. Hendrik Ezerman, *Managing Director*

Year Book 1935-1936

FIFTY-NINTH SEASON

Branch Schools

Oak Lane, Bank Building, 6701 N. Broad Street

Ardmore, Penna., The Rittenhouse, 52 East Lancaster Avenue

Alice E. Stallman   Mary V. Hagerty
Assistant Secretary   *Secretary*

THE PHILADELPHIA CONSERVATORY OF MUSIC

One of the oldest chartered music schools in the State of Pennsylvania

FIFTY-NINTH SEASON

While highly endowed institutions provide opportunities for a free musical education in the case of a limited number of outstanding talents, the task of offering a thorough musical training to the general public on a sane and sound basis cannot be neglected if music is to take its rightful place in the civic and national life of the United States.

Not only to teach professional players, but to start the musical training of children in the right way, to teach the layman to enjoy the art of music, to prepare capable teachers and give them a valuable musical background, is the aim of THE PHILADELPHIA CONSERVATORY OF MUSIC.

DEGREES

By virtue of the power granted to THE PHILADELPHIA CONSERVATORY OF MUSIC in its charter, the Philadelphia Conservatory is empowered by Article Second to "grant to its students diplomas of honorary testimonials in such form as it may designate, and grant and confer such honors, titles and degrees as are granted and conducted by any University in the United States for proficiency in music.

The three degrees conferred by this institution are: *Bachelor of Music*   *Master of Music*   *Doctor of Music*

SPECIAL COURSES

The Layman's Music Courses

By MME. OLGA SAMAROFF, Mus.D.

for

CONCERT AND OPERA-GOERS

RADIO LISTENERS

RECORD COLLECTORS

MUSICAL AMATEURS

who wish to extend and enrich their musical experience

LISTENING AS A MUSICAL ACTIVITY

The Initiation Course devised for the layman including:

Fundamentals of Music.

Ear-training.

Initiation into musical literature.

This course lasting twenty weeks is divided in two periods:

1. Eight weeks devoted primarily to the fundamentals of music and eartraining.

2. Twelve weeks devoted to an exploration of musical history and musical literature in the light of knowledge gained.

This entire course provides a weekly class of an hour in the subjects mentioned above and a weekly class of one hour in eartraining and theory. The hour classes include musical illustrations by means of records or competent performers.

The lessons in eartraining and theory according to a special method of presentation form a distinctive feature of these courses and have obtained remarkable results.

In addition to the classes outlined above the following courses are available:

1. An advanced course going more extensively into the subjects covered in the initiation course.

2. Courses for subscribers to concerts or opera.

3. Elective courses. A course on Bach, a course on Modern Music. etc.

A New Type of Private Music Lesson

In response to the increasing demand for a type of musical education that makes music a cultural part of life and develops the understanding listener, the Philadelphia Conservatory of Music announces, in addition to existing classes, a new type of private lesson in which the student can acquire familiarity with musical literature in conjunction with a knowledge of musical fundamentals.

For further information apply to the registrar.

Faculty

Pianoforte

MADAME OLGA SAMAROFF, Mus.D., Master Class
ARTHUR REGINALD, Graduate and Post Graduate Classes

WINIFRED ATKINSON	MARY ISAAC	ROBERT H. SLOAN, JR., Mus.M.
BRUCE C. BEACH, Mus.M.	KATHRINE LIPPINCOTT, Mus.B.	ROSALYN TURECK,
ALLISON R. DRAKE	MARY E. NAULTY, Mus.B.	Asst. to MME. SAMAROFF
MARIA EZERMAN DRAKE, Mus.B.	GLADYS E. JOHNSON	EDITH CAROLYN ULMER, Mus.B.
MAE E. HAINES	JANE PRICE	FLORENCE E. URBAN

Violin

BORIS KOUTZEN, Head of Department
CHARLTON LEWIS MURPHY

HELEN ROWLEY, Mus.B.   WILLIAM BLESS, JR., Mus.B.

Viola
GUSTAVE LOEBEN

Violoncello
STEPHEN DEAK

Voice

SUSANNA DERCUM   CLYDE R. DENGLER, B.S., A.M.
MAME E. ROTH   ESTHER M. TENNENT

Organ

By co-operative arrangements, instruction in organ will be given by the Kinder School, 217 South 20th St.

RALPH KINDER, Director

ALLISON R. DRAKE, Assistant

Harp

EDNA PHILLIPS, First Harpist of the Philadelphia Orchestra

Department of Musical Science and Composition
FREDERICK W. SCHLIEDER, Mus.D., F.A.G.O., Head of Department
KATHRYN R. GRUBE, Mus.B.

Class in Practical Orchestration
And in the Principles of Conducting
BRUCE C. BEACH, Mus.M.

Teachers' Training, Psychology and Pedagogy
WINIFRED ATKINSON

History of Music
CHARLTON LEWIS MURPHY

Ensemble Classes
ARTHUR REGINALD
BORIS KOUTZEN
CHARLTON LEWIS MURPHY
HELEN ROWLEY

Layman's Courses
MME. OLGA SAMAROFF, Mus.D.
ROSALYN TURECK

Orchestra of the Conservatory
BORIS KOUTZEN

Opera Class
JOHN A. THOMS, JR., Musical Director
KARL F. SCHROEDER, Stage Director

Flute
JOHN A. FISCHER

Horn
CLARENCE MAYER

Oboe and English Horn
ROBERT BLOOM

Trumpet
HAROLD W. REHRIC

Clarinet
FRED DIETRICHS

Trombone
FRED C. STOLL

Bassoon
HERMAN MUELLER

Timpani and Drum
EMIL KRESSE

OLGA SAMAROFF, Mus.D., holds the Master Class in piano in the Philadelphia Conservatory of Music. Her reputation as a pianist is international. As a writer on musical subjects and as a lecturer she is equally well known. Her outstanding work as a member of the staff of the post-graduate school of the Juilliard Foundation has placed her name among those of the world's most famous teachers.

ARTHUR REGINALD, Pianist, comes from a musical family. Mr. Reginald had his early musical training in the Middle West. Ii 1923 he entered the Juilliard Foundation Graduate School of New York, where he studied for five years with Madame Olga Samaroff. After that Mr. Reginald played in all the main cities of the eastern part of the United States as a soloist as well as taking part in chamber music concert programs. Being in charge of a large class of piano students at the conservatory, his work as a teacher speaks for itself.

The Philadelphia Conservatory announces the engagement of ROSALYN TURECK, winner of the 1935 New York State Liberty District, National Federation of Music Clubs and Schubert Memorial awards as a member of its piano faculty. Miss Tureck has held a fellowship for four years in the class of Madame Olga Samaroff at the Juilliard Graduate School of New York, where she has also successfully functioned as teacher of the composers, conductors and singers for whom the study of piano is obligatory in the Juilliard School. Before coming to New York, Miss Tureck studied with Herriot Levy and Chiapusso in Chicago where she made a deep impression in concert as a child prodigy. Miss Tureck who takes a great interest in educational work, will combine concertizing with her duties at the Philadelphia Conservatory of Music, where she will collaborate with her former teacher, Madame Olga Samaroff in the development of advanced pupils.

BORIS KOUTZEN, Violinist and Composer, was born in Uman, Russia. He entered the Moscow Imperial Conservatory, studying under Prof. Leo Zeitlin (violin) and Reingold Gliere (composition). After his graduation in 1922 he went to Germany to complete his studies. Mr. Koutzen gave numerous recitals and chamber music concerts in Europe as well as in America.

Of his compositions, the most important ones are: a Poeme-Nocturne, "Solitude" (performed by the Philadelphia and San Francisco orchestras), a Symphonic poem, "Valley Forge," Symphonic Movement for violin and orchestra. Trio for Flute, Cello and Harp, and a String quartet.

CHARLTON LEWIS MURPHY, Violinist and Lecturer, is a native of Philadelphia. His early training in violin and theory was obtained in the United States. Later he studied in Vienna under Jacob Grün and after several years with that celebrated pedagogue, won the Diplôme de Virtuosité at the Conservatoire de Genève under

Henri Marteau. Mr. Murphy is widely known as an educator through his constructive work in the National Association of Music Schools.

STEPHEN DEAK, Violincellist, was prepared for a professional career under the instruction of the great cellist David Popper at the Royal Hungarian Academy of Music in Budapest. In America, Mr. Deak studied with Felix Salmond, was a member of the Cincinnati Symphony and later of the Philadelphia Orchestra; Mr. Deak appeared as soloist in New York, Philadelphia, Baltimore, Washington, etc., and as a member of the Musical Fund Quartet took a major part in the Brahms Centenary series of Chamber Music Concerts, which were given in Philadelphia during the winter of 1933. Mr. Deak is the author of the "Modern Method for the Violincello," which is recognized by critics as an extraordinary work among modern pedagogical literature.

FREDERICK W. SCHLIEDER, Mus.D., F.A.G.O., head of the Department of Theory of Music, returned from abroad in 1927, having made Paris his temporary home for a considerable period of time. While in the latter city, Mr. Schlieder has given successful courses in his field of instruction and has concentrated his efforts on assembling his unique and valuable ideas in book form for publication. (Lyric Composition through Improvisation). Mr. Schlieder instructs his classes in musical science and composition on a creative basis.

EDNA PHILLIPS, first Harpist of the Philadelphia Orchestra, who studied with Carlos Salezdo at the Curtis Institute of Music in Philadelphia, is a soloist of high standing, a thorough musician and an enthusiastic teacher of her beloved instrument. Miss Phillips is one of the three harpists who compiled a four year course in Harp, to be used for credit in High Schools.

SUSANNA DERCUM was born in Philadelphia and had her early voice training with Nicholas Douty in that city.

Later Miss Dercum studied in Berlin, Germany, under Clara Willenbucher, who was for years the assistant to Lily Lehman.

After returning to America, Miss Dercum went on a concert tour with John McCormick and was later engaged by Leopold Stokowski to be one of the soloists in the American Premier of Mahler's Eighth Symphony.

Miss Dercum has given Lieder Recitals for numerous societies in Philadelphia, Boston, Newark and Washington and in many colleges.

CLYDE R. DENGLER, B.S., A.M., studied voice in Philadelphia with Nicholas Douty and Warren Shaw, in New York with Isadore Luckstone. Mr. Dengler received a Fellowship in voice at the Juilliard Graduate School of New York under Schoen-Rene.

He received the degree of Bachelor of Science and the degree of Master of Arts from the University of Pennsylvania.

Advantages of The Philadelphia Conse

In the Conservatory Department courses of study are provided for each branch of musical art, including everything necessary for the training of an artist, a teacher or any serious amateur student of music. These courses, none of which should be neglected, correlate and amplify each other, with the one object in view, viz.: a thorough, well balanced musical education. Teachers of the best quality only, each selected for excellence in his special field, are in charge of their special courses of instruction.

In the Preparatory Department meticulous attention is given to students beginning their musical education. The responsibility of starting the child's musical training in the right way rests with the parents, whose attention therefore is invited to the efficient system of grading and requirements, examinations and degrees outlined under the heading: Schools for Piano, Violin and Theory of Music. This system, THE PHILADELPHIA CONSERVATORY SYSTEM, is bound to lead to a maximum of progress and efficiency. Through this system the ambition of the student is aroused and steadily maintained. New students desiring to enter the Conservatory will know instantly how they can be placed and what

CONCERT and COMMENCEMENT
1934-1935
Wednesday Evening, May 22, 1935
8.15 O'CLOCK PRECISELY
BELLEVUE-STRATFORD BALL ROOM
Broad and Walnut Streets
PROGRAM

Concerto C major for two pianos and string orchestra
1st movement .... *Bach*
  Mary Gorin   Arnold Fletcher

Introduction and Rondo Capriccioso.................. *Saint-Saens*
    Edward B. Haines
   Edith C. Ulmer at the Piano

Introduction and Allegro for harp with flute, clarinet and
string orchestra .... *Ravel*
 Harp—C. Louise Zehring Flute—L. Jeanne Russell
   Conservatory String Orchestra

Piano Group—Nocturne, B major .... *Chopin*
   Alice B. Davis

   Rhapsodie, G minor .... *Brahms*
   Frances Ferdman

   Ritmo .....:........................... *Infante*
   Alice B. Davis, Jane M. Kolb

En Bateau .... *Debussy*
   Conservatory Orchestra

Concerto for piano, violin and string orchestra, 1st movement *Chausson*
 Piano—Janet Dickson Violin—Helen Weisz
   Conservatory String Orchestra

Concerto G major for piano .... *Ravel*
  Ethel Selnick, 1st movement
  Eugene List, 2nd and 3rd movements
PRESENTATION OF DIPLOMAS AND DEGREES
COMMENCEMENT EXERCISES CONDUCTED BY
MME. OLGA SAMAROFF, Mus.D.

RESUME OF ACTIVITIES

Eleven Closed Concerts by students of the Preparatory and Conservatory Departments.

Two Sunday afternoon Concerts for children at the Conservatory, on January 20, and March 31, 1935.

Piano Recital by Arthur Reginald at Mount Saint Joseph's, Chestnut Hill, November 21, 1934.

Chamber Music Program, on Tuesday, December 11, 1934, at The Presser Home, Germantown, Phila.

Musical Program, Christmas Meeting of The Fellowship of The Philadelphia Conservatory of Music, December 20, 1934.

Two Piano Recital by Maria Ezerman Drake and Allison R. Drake, at the Ethical Society Auditorium, April 15, 1935.

Illustrated Lecture by Clyde Dengler, on "Is There Radio and Recording Technique?" April 7, 1935.

Recital by Vocal Pupils of Susanna Dercum assisted by the Philcon Instrumental Ensemble, May 1, 1935.

Recital of Original Compositions by Students of the Composition Classes, under the direction of Frederick W. Schlieder, Mus.D., at the Art Alliance, May 2, 1935.

Demonstration by students of the Preparatory Department under the direction of Miss Kathryn R. Grube, Mus.B., June 6, 1935.

"A Musical Revue" under the direction of Paul Nordoff, May 4, 1935.

Piano Recital by Katherine Lippincott at the Ethical Society Auditorium, May 8, 1935.

Violin Recital by Helen Weisz, May 10, 1935.

Concert and Commencement, the Bellevue-Stratford Ball-room, May 22, 1935.

A Special Children's Concert, Ethical Society Auditorium, June 8, 1935.

Advanced Students' Concert, Ethical Society Auditorium, June 13, 1935.

Schools for Piano, Violin and Musical Science

Three Main Departments: *I, Preparatory Course; II, Conservatory Course,* leading to Teacher's Diploma; *III, Post Graduate Course (Master Class),* leading to Soloist Diploma and Degrees.

Approximate outline of material used for study in the different grades and statement of requirements for examinations, which enable students to pass into a higher grade.

1. PREPARATORY COURSE

This Course is divided into six grades: Elementary Course A, I, II and III; and Elementary Course B, I, II and III

N. B.—The letters P. S. C. refer to the Progressive Series Catalog, edited by the Art Publications Society, in St. Louis. Numbers refer to the same Catalog. Most of the numbers have been edited by Leopold Godowsky.

PIANO
ELEMENTARY A, I, II AND III

Exercises.   P. S. C. Nos. 5, 8, 11, 12, 13, 15, or equivalents. Beginning of scale work: C and G major, A and E minor.

Studies.   Early studies from Kroeger, Streabbog, Heller, etc. (See P. S. C. Grades 1A, 1B, 2A.) Especially advised: Nos. 315, 316, 317, 318.

Pieces.   From P. S. C. Grades 1A, 1B, 2A. Especially advised: Educational adaptations by L. Godowsky. P. S. C. French Suite 307, Swedish Suite 308, Hungarian Suite 342, or equivalent.

VIOLIN
ELEMENTARY A, I, II AND III

Exercises.   Joachim and Moser: Violin School, first volume (for beginners). Beginning of scale work. (J. Hrimaly).

Studies.   Beginning of F. Wohlfahrt Op. 45.

Pieces.   Hoffman Op. 85: 16 melodious pieces. 25 pieces in the first position (Schirmer). Other pieces of similar difficulty.

1. PREPARATORY COURSE. Continued

PIANO
ELEMENTARY B, I, II AND III

Exercises. P. S. C. Nos. 49, 52, 53, 54, 55, 56, 57, 58, 59, 60. Nos. 16, 17, 19, 20, 21, 23, 24 (Godowsky, Schmidt, etc.).
Major and Minor scales through 4 sharps and 4 flats, arpeggios.

Studies. From Bertini Op. 100, Streabbog Op. 64, Heller, etc. (See P. S. C. Grades 2A, 2B, 3A.)
Bach for beginners. Bach Vincent. Bach Carroll or equivalents.

Pieces. From P. S. C. Grades 2A, 2B, 3A.
Especially advised: Little Hedge Rose by Schubert-Godowsky (446), Ruthenian Melodies (443), Sonatina in F by Beethoven (427), or equivalents.

EXAMINATION

Scales and arpeggios.

Studies. Duvernoy Op. 120, No. 7 (520), Burgmueller Op. 105, No. 3 (510), Bertini Op. 100, No. 12 (504), or equivalent.
Bach from material suggested above.

Pieces. Sonatina by Beethoven in F or in G (obligatory). Three other pieces.

VIOLIN
ELEMENTARY B, I, II AND III

Exercises. Beginning of double stops in the first position (Violin School by Joachim and Moser, volume 2, Nos. 10-37).
Exercises for second and third positions (Joachim and Moser, volume 2, Nos. 38-118).
Scales: J. Hrimaly, scales in the first position.

Studies. Selected from Wohlfahrt Op. 45.

Pieces. Concertinos by A. Huber, easier Concertinos by Seitz, Airs varies by C. Dancla, Opera fantasies by J. B. Singelee.

EXAMINATION

Major and minor scales.

Studies. Etudes by Wohlfahrt (Nos. 43, 46, 49, 51, 53, 54 preferred).

Pieces. Two pieces from material suggested above.

The length of time necessary for the completion of this course cannot be stated definitely, as age, general education and musical conception of the student are all important factors involved.

2. CONSERVATORY COURSE. This Course is divided into six grades: Junior Course A and B, Senior Course A and B, Graduate Course A and B

PIANO
JUNIOR COURSE A, I AND II

Exercises.   Scales and arpeggios with cadences, thirds and sixths, trills, repeated notes, etc. (See P. S. C.)

Studies.   From Czerny Op. 636, Bertini, Heller, etc. (P. S. C. Grades 3A, 3B, 4A).
Bach: Two or three two-part inventions (Bach-Busoni).

Pieces.   Sonatas by Mozart in C or G. Sonatas by Beethoven, G major, G minor, Op. 49.
Durand's Chaconne, Chopin's valses in A minor or B minor (635-634) or equivalents. (See P. S. C. Grades 3A, 3B.)

ANNUAL EXAMINATION
Scales and arpeggios with cadences.

Studies.   Three.
Bach: Two-part invention No. 4.

Pieces.   Two from material suggested above.

VIOLIN
JUNIOR COURSE A, I AND II

Exercises.   Scales, Hrimaly; exercises in the fourth, fifth, sixth and seventh positions (material to be selected from Joachim and Moser, volume 2, part 2); Sevcik Op. 3, exercises for the bow; Schradieck, school for violin technic, part 1

Studies   Selected from H. E. Kayser Op. 20 and F. Mazas Op. 36 first book; Hofmann Op. 96, double stop studies.

Pieces   More difficult concertinos by Seitz; Concerto by Accolay; Opera fantasies by Singelee; Arc. Corelli, 15 pieces (Corelli album, Ed. Litolff).

ANNUAL EXAMINATION
Major and minor scales in two octaves (No. 7 from Hrimaly).

Studies.   Mazas (Nos. 19, 20, 23, 25, 26, 28 preferred. Ed. Fisher).

Pieces.   Two pieces from material suggested above.

2. CONSERVATORY COURSE. Continued

PIANO

Exercises. As before, but extended.

Studies. As before, also Cramer, Clementi. (See P. S. C. Grades 4A, 4B.)
Bach: Two part inventions.

Pieces. Haydn Sonata D major, Beethoven Op. 2, No. 1, Mozart's Fantasy in D minor (602), Schubert's Impromptu in A flat (808), or equivalents. (See P. S. C. Grades 4A, 4B.)

ANNUAL EXAMINATION
Scales, etc.

Studies. Two.
Bach: Two-part invention No. 9.

Pieces. Beethoven Sonata Op. 2 No. 1, first two movements. Two other pieces from material suggested above.

VIOLIN
JUNIOR COURSE B, I AND II

Exercises. Scales, Hrimaly; Sevcik Op. 8 (exercise for the changing of positions); Schradieck, school for violin technic, part 2.

Studies. Mazas Op. 36, second book; Dont Op. 37.

Pieces. Concerto Op. 31 by Hans Sitt; Second Concertino Op. 14 by Rene Ortmans; Concerto No. 4 by Rode; Airs varies by De Beriot and other pieces of similar difficulty.

ANNUAL EXAMINATION
Scales in two octaves.

Studies. From Dont Op. 37.

Pieces. Two compositions from material suggested above.

2. CONSERVATORY COURSE, Continued

PIANO
SENIOR COURSE A

Exercises. Extended (Octaves, chords, etc. See P. S. C.).

Studies. Czerny Op. 740, Gramer, Clementi, etc. (Grade 5A P. S. C.).
Bach: Two and three-part inventions.

Pieces. Beethoven Sonatas Op. 2, No. 1, last movement, and Op. 14, No. 2; Mozart Concerto, one movement; other pieces, such as Schumann's Novelettes in B minor Op. 99 (904), in F major (914); also easier modern compositions by Debussy, Scott, Rachmaninoff, or others. (See P. S. C. Grades 4B, 5A).

ANNUAL EXAMINATION
Scales, etc.

Studies. Two from Czerny Op. 740 Nos. 3 and 23 preferred.
Bach: Three-part invention No. 7.

Pieces. Beethoven Sonata, like Op. 14 No. 2, two movements. Two other pieces from material suggested above.

VIOLIN
SENIOR COURSE A

Exercises. Scales in three octaves, Hrimaly No. 10.
Sevcik Op. 1, parts 3 and 4.

Studies. R. Kreutzer.

Pieces. Concertos by Rode (choice of Nos. 1, 7, 8); De Beriot (choice of Nos. 1, 7, 9); Kreutzer No. 19, Viotti No. 23; Handel Sonata in D or in E. Concert pieces like Scene de Ballet by De Beriot.

ANNUAL EXAMINATION
Scales in three octaves.

Studies. Kreutzer Nos. 8, 12, 14, 20, 22, 24, 28, 30, 31, 35.

Pieces. Two compositions from material suggested above. Handel Sonata, obligatory.

2. CONSERVATORY COURSE. Continued

PIANO
Senior Course B

Exercises. Extended, miscellaneous, see P. S. C. (Godowsky).

Studies. As before, extended and selected.
Bach: Three-part inventions, also parts of suites.

Pieces. Beethoven Sonatas, not from last period; Mozart Concerto.
Pieces such as Chopin's C sharp minor Polonaise (915),
Andante con Variazioni by Haydn (1105). (See P. S.
C. Grades 4A, 4B, 5A.)

Annual Examination
Scales, etc.

Studies. Two.
Bach: Three-part inventions, Nos. 3 and 15.

Pieces. Beethoven Sonata, two movements and two other compositions from material suggested above.

VIOLIN
Senior Course B

Exercises. Scales in three octaves and double stops. Sevcik Op. 1,
part 4 (like before but extended).

Studies. Selected from Fiorillo; Rode, 24 Caprices.

Pieces. Concertos: Viotti No. 22; Spohr Nos. 2 or 11; Lipinski;
Bach Concerto Nos. 1 or 2. Old Masters ("Die Hohe
Schule des Violinspiels" arranged, and edited by David).

Annual Examination
Scales in three octaves, double stops

Studies. Four selected from Fiorillo and Rode.

Pieces. Concertos: Viotti or Spohr; Bach Concerto (obligatory).
Movement of a Sonata by one of the old masters.

2. CONSERVATORY COURSE. Continued

PIANO
GRADUATE COURSE A

Exercises. Scales in double thirds and sixths, miscellaneous, see P. S. C. (Godowsky).

Studies. Extended, more difficult. Beginning of Chopin studies, carefully selected.

Bach: Three-part inventions, beginning of Well Tempered Clavichord.

Pieces. Beethoven Sonatas, like before, carefully selected. Selected compositions by Chopin, Schumann, Moszkowski, Liszt, Rachmaninoff, Debussy, etc. Mozart Concerto.

ANNUAL EXAMINATION

Scales in double thirds and sixths.
Bach: Three-part inventions Nos. 9 and 14.
Beethoven Sonata, like Op. 27, No. 1.
A Chopin Nocturne, and a lighter composition, more brilliant.

VIOLIN
GRADUATE COURSE A I and II

Exercises. Covering the entire violin technic selected from material mentioned before and arranged for daily use.

Studies. Rovelli, 12 Etudes. Gavinies, 24 Matinees.

Repertoire. Concertos: Mozart; Spohr, Nos. 8 or 9; Bruch; Mendelssohn. Tartini Sonata. Vitaly Ciaconna. Concert pieces by Vieuxtemps (Ballade and Polonaise, Fantasia Appassionata).

ANNUAL EXAMINATION

Studies. Two selected from Gavinies.

Repertoire. Concertos: Spohr and Mozart (obligatory). Concert piece by Vieuxtemps or something equally difficult.

PIANO

GRADUATE COURSE B

Studies. As before, also three Chopin Etudes. Review Czerni, Clementi.
Bach: Well Tempered Clavichord.

Repertoire. Concertos: Beethoven C minor; Mendelssohn C minor, or Grieg, etc. One to be selected. Other selected compositions, including the more modern composers.

FINAL EXAMINATION

Technical Part. Three Chopin Etudes.
Ability to play fluently studies by Czerni and Clementi.
Bach: Two Preludes and Fugues.

Repertoire. Beethoven Sonata, not from the last period. A Movement of a Concerto. Three recital compositions, one of the student's own choice.

VIOLIN

GRADUATE COURSE B I and II

Studies. Dont Op. 35. Review: Kreutzer, Rode.
Bach: Sonatas for violin solo.

Repertoire. Beethoven Concerto; one of the Vieuxtemps Concertos; concert pieces like Polonaise by Wieniawski.

FINAL EXAMINATION

Technical Part. Two studies by Dont. Ability to play fluently studies by Kreutzer and Rode.
Bach: Movement of one of the Sonatas for violin solo.

Repertoire. A Movement of a Concerto (Beethoven or Mendelssohn preferred). Concerto or concert piece by Vieuxtemps. 3 concert pieces, one of student's own choice, (studied without the aid of the teacher).

In the Conservatory Course every student is advised to take the annual examination, regardless of the progress that has been made. In case of failure to pass the examination, the examiners may set a date for a new trial, thereby offering another chance to succeed by means of increased effort. A more or less advanced student, entering the Conservatory, will be graded by the instructor according to ability shown during the first period of instruction.

3. POST GRADUATE COURSE. (Master Class), leading to Soloist Diploma and Degrees

PIANO

Repertoire. Bach: Original works and arrangements from the organ by Liszt, Tausig, Busoni, etc.

Beethoven: Sonatas from the last period.

Concertos: Beethoven, Chopin, Schumann, Liszt, Brahms, Tschaikowsky, etc.

Recital pieces covering the entire literature, also modern composers.

Chopin and Liszt Etudes.

EXAMINATION

Public recital, which must contain: Bach, Beethoven, well chosen recital pieces.

VIOLIN

Repertoire. Bach: Sonatas for violin solo.

Concert pièces.

Concertos: Paganini, Ernst, Brahms, Wieniawski, Tschaikowsky, Lalo, Glasounoff, etc.

Caprices and Concert Etudes by Paganini, Wieniawski, etc.

EXAMINATION

Public recital, which must contain: a Sonata for piano and violin; a Bach Sonata for violin solo; a Concerto; a group of smaller compositions.

HARP

Repertoire. Peschetti, Sonata; Handel, The Hamonious Blacksmith; Gluck, Gavotte from Armide; Salzedo, Flight; In Quietude; Idyllic Poem; DeBussy, La Fille aux Cheveux the Lin; Palmgren, May Night (transcription by Florence Wrightman); DeBussy, En Bateau; Salzedo, Variations in G; Ravel, Introduction et Allegro, or, DeBussy, Danses Sacree et Profane.

EXAMINATION

Public recital.

The Annual Examinations, mentioned in the Conservatory Course, do not concern students of the Master Class. At the examination of the latter the public will be invited.

Department of Musical Science and Composition

ELEMENTARY COURSE

INTERMEDIATE COURSE

COURSE LEADING TO TEACHER'S DIPLOMA AND BACHELOR OF MUSIC
DEGREE

First Year. Harmony I

Notation, Scales, Intervals, Triads, Cadences, Figured
Basses employing Triads and Seventh Chord and their
Inversions. Harmonization of Melodies. Analysis.

Lyric Composition I

Keyboard Harmony and Improvization with special
emphasis on phrasing and form, from the beginning;
Exercises employing Triads, Inversions, and Seventh
Chords in close and open position; Harmonization of
original melodies, Rhythm drills, Modulation in Harmonic embellishments, Figuration. Practical composition in the smaller forms.

Second Year. Harmony II

Two and Three Part Counterpoint.

Its application to the Suite and Invention.

Third Year. Four Part Counterpoint and Fugue.

Fourth Year. Lyric Composition II, III, IV, V, VI, VII

(Pianistic types of Musical Composition.)

Rondo Form; Sonata Form.

Analysis of, and Composition in the larger Forms.

COURSE LEADING TO THE MASTER OF MUSIC DEGREE

(As a Continuation of the Bachelor Degree)

Two Years

ORCHESTRATION

Original Composition
Non-original Composition } Elective
Choral Composition with Orchestra

LECTURES

Musical Philosophy
Musical Psychology

THESIS

NOTE: Students in departments other than piano may be exempt from Lyric II, III, IV and V by substituting two years of piano study.

In reference to students transferring from other institutions, to qualify for candidacy for the Bachelor's Degree will require from one to two years, depending upon the applicant's eligibility on entrance, which eligibility shall be determined by faculty examination.

SPECIAL COURSES

Courses for Special Students are available in this Department either in Class or Privately

Requirements for Teacher's Diploma

PIANO

Successful completion of the Graduate Course B, as outlined on page 17
Solfeggio 1, 2 and 3
History 1
History 2 and appreciation of music
Orchestration 1
Orchestration 2
Teachers' training 1
Teachers' training 2
Psychology and pedagogy
Ensemble Class, a minimum of two years
Musical science and composition—1, 2, and 3 page 19)

VIOLIN

Successful completion of the Graduate Course B, as outlined on page 17
Solfeggio 1, 2 and 3
History 1
History 2 and appreciation of music
Orchestration 1
Orchestration 2
Teachers' training 1
Psychology and pedagogy
Ensemble Class, a minimum of two years
Musical science and composition—1, 2, and 3 (page 19)
Orchestra Class, during the entire Conservatory course
Completion of Piano Elementary B III

HARP

Two Etudes from Salzedo's modern method for harp:
Bach, Bourree; Corelli, Giga; Haydn Theme and variations.
Ravel: Introduction et Allegro, or De Bussy: Danses Sacree et Profrane.
DeBussy, En Bateau. Choice of Faure Impromptu, or, Gareil Pierni, Impromptu Caprice.
Associate subjects as required in the course for organ.

ORGAN

Examinations
One of the larger fugues by Bach (G minor, A minor or D minor), a sonata by Mendelssohn and an extended composition by a modern composer, as, for instance, the D minor sonata of Guilmant, one of the organ symphonies of Widor, etc. The applicant will also be required to accompany any of the Hymns, Canticles and Anthems used in the Episcopal service; to transpose a hymn tune after playing it through in the original key, and to answer simple questions about the construction of the organ.
Solfeggio 1, 2 and 3
History 1
History 2 and appreciation of music
Orchestration 1
Orchestration 2
Teachers' training 1
Psychology and pedagogy
Musical science and composition—1, 2 and 3 (page 19)
Secondary piano
Choir training

'CELLO

Examinations
A suite by Bach for 'cello solo, a concerto (Haydn, Dvorak, Lalo or Schumann), three concert pieces, one of which must be the student's own choice.
Associate subjects as required in the course for violin.

VOICE

Examinations
An aria from the Standard Oratorios.
An aria from the standard operas. A song or aria by one of the older composers: Scarlatti, Gluck, Haydn, Mozart, etc.
Two songs from the Romantic School: Schubert, Schumann, Frantz. One modern song.
Associate subjects as required in the course for organ
Operatic training.

Requirements for Degrees

Awarding of the **Degree of Bachelor** will not only depend upon playing ability, but also on the high standing of the student in all branches pertaining to the art of music in its highest form. In addition to the requirements for the Teachers' Diploma (page 21) candidates for the Bachelor Degree of Music are required to complete the Fourth Year of the Course in Musical Science and Composition (page 19) and to study a minimum of one year, the instrument in which they major.

Applicants for the **Degree of Master of Music** must have had at least two years of practical musical experience after having been awarded the degree of Bachelor of Music. Two years of study is required for the degree, Master of Music, one of which must be in residence. (page 20).

The theoretical requirements for the Master Degree depend upon whether Composition is taken as the major or secondary subject.

If the major subject, original compositions for strings, chorus and orchestra in the larger forms are required.

If the secondary subject the requirements are:

Original compositions for the instrument in which the candidate is majoring, four-voice fugue, vocal or instrumental and scoring a composition for orchestra.

In addition a recital program must be played on the instrument in which the candidate is majoring.

For the **Soloist Diploma** the student must complete the entire teachers' course and the post graduate course in the instrument in which he majors, at the end of which a public recital will be required.

Prizes and Scholarships

In case of extraordinary talent, a Free Scholarship, either entirely or partially, may be awarded by the Conservatory to the student who does not possess the means of defraying the expenses of the course.

The D. Hendrik Ezerman Foundation scholarship for a talented and worthy piano student under Madame Olga Samaroff's personal instruction will be awarded for the season 1935-1936 in open competition in the last week of September. Requirements and definite details concerning this scholarship may be secured at the office.

THE FELLOWSHIP OF THE PHILADELPHIA CONSERVATORY OF MUSIC is an organization of some of the advanced students of the Conservatory and members of the Faculty, for the joint study, appreciation and performance of music in all its phases.

This year the Fellowship is awarding two scholarships in ensemble playing to students who excelled in general standing, in character and helpfulness.

The Hood Scholarship in piano has been awarded for the season 1935-1936 to Mary Gorin.

Concerts and Recitals

Besides the regular student concerts a number of Faculty Concerts and Lectures will be given for the educational value to the student body. It is obligatory to all regular course students in the grades Senior B, Graduate A and Graduate B to attend all the Faculty Concerts and Lectures and at least fifty per cent of the student recitals.

THE VOCAL DEPARTMENT INTRODUCES
A NEW METHOD IN VOICE TEACHING

Vocal concepts based on adequate terminology and new measuring devices.

Recordings of the pupil's voice are made periodically.

This gives the student and teacher an authentic history of development. It also gives the student an opportunity to hear himself, making the singing processes more objective.

A study of vowels and their analysis to fundamental sounds.

This is made very interesting through the use of an electric vowel box.

Vowel color and fundamental sounds as seen in the cattiode ray oscillograph in the Franklin Institute and the new vocal analyzer of the Moore Scientific School, University of Pennsylvania.

Application of psychological principles in the study of voice chiefly as they apply to the voluntary and reflex muscular mechanism.

The final objective, a good singing voice, emancipated from the teacher through a thorough understanding of the scientific principles involved in voice production.

Classes in correct speech will be given.

COURSE IN PRACTICAL ORCHESTRATION
By Bruce Cresswell Beach, Mus.M.

A course designed to meet the practical needs of professional musicians, music teachers, and orchestra and band leaders. Emphasis to be laid on the every-day practical use of the instruments, with demonstrations on each instrument as it is studied. Full-scores of works by well-known composers, and phonograph recordings of these works, will be studied.

Subjects to be included:

The evolution of the modern orchestra

Ranges and technical possibilities of the instruments

Full-score writing

Harmonic texture, as applied to instrumental writing

Arranging for small groups of instruments

The possibilities of the symphonic band

A study of modernistic tendencies

COURSE IN CONDUCTING

Principles of baton technique; problems in interpretation; advanced problems in orchestration and arranging; score-reading and writing; discussions of individual problems.

Opera Class

The Opera Class is conducted by Mr. John A. Thoms, Jr., Musical Director, and Mr. Karl T. F. Schroeder, Stage Director.

Mr. Thoms is Musical Director of the Savoy Co., Philadelphia Operatic Society, and Mozart Opera Co. of Philadelphia.

Mr. Schroeder is Stage Manager of the Robin Hood Dell Opera Co., was formerly with the Metropolitan Opera Co., New York, Philadelphia Grand and Civic Opera Co.

Besides operatic training, coaching in dramatic and operatic roles may be subscribed for either privately or in class.

For detailed information apply at the office of the Conservatory.

History I

is an intensive, detailed study of the History and Development of Music from the earliest beginnings to the complexities of modern structure. The student is given a comprehensive background of relative historical and cultural events, that enriches his understanding of the progress of his particular art. To stimulate a lively interest in the subject matter and to acquire a definite working knowledge of historical accuracy is the immediate goal of the course.

History II

is a more intimate study of composers and their works, emphasizing the periods of composition. Appreciation of Music and Intelligent Listening are a regular part of the class routine. Compositions, instrumental and vocal, are given in the class, explanatory to the History of Material and Form of Musical Compositions. A study of the Orchestra, its music and instruments and the characteristic features of the various periods in its history, constitutes a major portion of this course destined to incite the student to a deeper study of the masters.

Choral Club

A weekly class in chorus singing will be conducted by Dr. Schlieder. These chorus practice periods, supplementary to the study and practice of Harmony and Counterpoint, are carried on in order that the inner sense and feeling of Harmonic and Contrapuntal movement may be developed more directly by an active vocal expression.

Orchestra and Ensemble Classes of the Conservatory

The Orchestra consists of pupils of the Conservatory. Rehearsals take place once a week. Different forms of Orchestral compositions will be rehearsed. Thus the pupils have every advantage for thorough drill in orchestral work.

The study of chamber music takes a very important part in our plan of musical education. This form of musical performance should be one of the aims of musical education and should be developed at an early stage. It is the art of giving and receiving. Self expression depends entirely upon the keenest ability to listen to others as well as to one's self.

Heretofore the privilege of Ensemble Playing has been reserved for those who were sufficiently advanced for the purpose of interpreting the works of the great masters. It is the aim of an ideal musical education, as it will be our aim, to start the study of the art of Ensemble Playing at the earliest possible moment.

The Teachers' Training Class

The Teacher's Training Class covers two years of study. The first year, the course consists of thirty lectures, each one hour in length. The Progressive Series of Piano Lessons will be used as the text and the entire Junior Course, covering the Elementary Grade, will be completed.

In the second year the course consists of thirty lessons, of one and a half hours' duration, each lesson combining Theory and Practice.

Practice teaching is done by class members. (Special attention in this course is also given to the study of teaching material.)

In connection with the practical work of the teachers' training course, a class is given in psychology covering 30 lessons of one hour each. The student is taught the theory of child training, involving an understanding of such factors in the work as interest, attention, method, instincts, habit, memory. This systematic method of study instills self-reliance into the students and prepares them in every way to enter the profession as efficient teachers.

Department of Solfeggio

A course is offered especially designed to meet the needs of the music student in ear training, sight reading, rhythmic development and elementary theory.

The subject matter of music is presented first to the sense of hearing whereby the student gains power to think tones and to sense rhythm, thereby learning to recognize and write simple melodic phrases in all keys.

Proficiency in sight reading is one of the greatest essentials in the study of music. All students are required to follow this course. Exceptions will be made only in the case of students who, after due examination, show sufficient ability to be excused from attending the course.

Tuition Fees

All tuition fees are due and payable in advance. The Conservatory year consists of forty teaching weeks, divided in three groups:

September 16—January 6 (16 weeks)
January 6—March 30 (12 weeks)
March 30—June 22 (12 weeks)

First payment 40% of the entire amount due September 16, 1935. Second payment 30% of the entire amount due January 6, 1935, and third payment 30% of the entire amount due April 1, 1935.

PIANO

Elementary Course, Junior Grades
Half-hour lessons, once a week, season $40.00, $60.00, $80.00

Conservatory Course, Senior and Graduate Grades
Half-hour lessons, once a week, per season...$80.00 to $200.00

Madame Samaroff's Post Graduate Course (Master Class)
Half-hour lessons, once a week, per person...........$400.00

VIOLIN

Elementary Course, Junior Grades
Half-hour lessons, once a week, season, $40.00, $60.00, $80.00

Conservatory Course, Senior and Graduate Grades
Half-hour lessons, once a week, per season...$80.00 to $160.00

Post Graduate Course (Master Class)
Half-hour lessons, once a week, per season...........$200.00

VIOLONCELLO
Lessons, once a week ....$100.00 to $200.00

ORGAN
Lessons, once a week, per season.........$100.00 to $160.00

VOICE CULTURE
Lessons, once a week, per season.........$100.00 to $200.00

HARP
Lessons once a week, per season.........$200.00 to $400.00

BAND AND ORCHESTRAL INSTRUMENTS
(Flute, Clarinet, Bassoon, Oboe, Trumpet, Trombone, etc.)
Half-hour lessons, once a week, per person..$60.00 to $160.00

DEPARTMENT OF MUSICAL SCIENCE AND COMPOSITION, THEORY OF MUSIC, SOLFEGGIO
Special arrangements may be made for private lessons with Dr. Schlieder and Miss Grube.

SOLFEGGIO

For regular students of the Conservatory,
  per season $20.00

DEPARTMENT OF MUSICAL SCIENCE AND COMPOSITION

Elementary and Junior Grades, per season.... 20.00
Senior and Graduates Grades, per season....... 60.00

PRACTICAL ORCHESTRATION CLASS

Per season 30.00

TEACHERS' TRAINING CLASS

First year, per season...................... 30.00
Second year, per season.................... 30.00
Class in Psychology and Pedagogy........... 30.00

MUSICAL HISTORY AND APPRECIATION OF MUSIC

Per season 25.00

THE LAYMAN'S MUSIC COURSES

Entire Course 35.00

ENSEMBLE CLASS

Per season 25.00

CHORAL CLASS

Per season 10.00

OPERA CLASS

Per season 10.00

ORCHESTRA CLASS

Per season 10.00
  Teacher's Diploma $20.00
  Soloist's Diploma 20.00
  Degrees 25.00

CALENDAR FOR THE SEASON 1934-1935

Registration Days On and After September 3rd

First term (16 weeks), Monday, September 16th to January 6th

Second term (12 weeks)........January 6th to March 30th

Third term (12 weeks)...........March 30th to June 22nd

Special Summer Term—June 29th August 8th

Pupils whose lessons fall on Holidays may arrange for these lessons at mutual convenience.

All classes in Theory, Harmony, Solfeggio, History, etc., will start on October 1st.

The Philadelphia Conservatory of Music uses
Steinway Pianos and Lyon and Healy Harps

The Conservatory Will Open for Enrollment of Pupils on Tuesday, September 3, 1935

Rules and Regulations

Beginners as well as advanced students may enter the Conservatory. No previous knowledge is required for admission.

Pupils may enroll at any time during the season, but, to insure greater efficiency in study, a course of 40 weeks, beginning September 16th, is recommended.

All arrangements as to lessons, payments, purchase of music, and business of all kinds, must be made with the Secretary of the Conservatory only. The Conservatory Office is open from 9.00 A. M. to 5.30 P. M.

ALL STUDENTS ENTERING THE CONSERVATORY
PLEDGE THEMSELVES TO LOYAL
OBSERVANCE OF THE FOLLOWING RULES

The Tuition Fee must be paid strictly in advance.

Pupils who are more than fifteen minutes late for any lesson forfeit the lesson. Punctuality is a necessity.

No pupil of the Conservatory is allowed to omit lessons without sufficient cause. Lessons lost in consequence of absence of students cannot be made good by the Con-

servatory. The teachers' hours are arranged for by the season, and they are in attendance whether the pupils are present or absent. In case of prolonged illness or other uncontrollable contingency, a special arrangement must be made.

Regular pupils of the Conservatory must, when called upon, participate in students' recitals and examinations, unless excused therefrom by their teachers and the Director. The importance of this rule is apparent: progress can be definitely observed and officially stated.

Pupils must refrain from whispering or other disturbing behaviour at concerts, lectures, etc.

Pupils are not permitted to take part in concerts outside of the Conservatory without the approval of their teachers.

The presentation of flowers at the students' concerts is not permitted.

Loud conversation, noise and laughter in the corridors are forbidden.

Pupils must examine the notices on the bulletin boards. Failure to do this results in many misunderstandings and disappointments.

The Conservatory Will Open for Enrollment of Pupils on Tuesday, September 3, 1935

· Rules and Regulations

Beginners as well as advanced students may enter the Conservatory. No previous knowledge is required for admission.

Pupils may enroll at any time during the season, but, to insure greater efficiency in study, a course of 40 weeks, beginning September 16th, is recommended.

All arrangements as to lessons, payments, purchase of music, and business of all kinds, must be made with the Secretary of the Conservatory only. The Conservatory Office is open from 9.00 A. M. to 5.30 P. M.

ALL STUDENTS ENTERING THE CONSERVATORY
PLEDGE THEMSELVES TO LOYAL
OBSERVANCE OF THE FOLLOWING RULES

The Tuition Fee must be paid strictly in advance.

Pupils who are more than fifteen minutes late for any lesson forfeit the lesson. Punctuality is a necessity.

No pupil of the Conservatory is allowed to omit lessons without sufficient cause. Lessons lost in consequence of absence of students cannot be made good by the Con-

servatory. The teachers' hours are arranged for by the season, and they are in attendance whether the pupils are present or absent. In case of prolonged illness or other uncontrollable contingency, a special arrangement must be made.

Regular pupils of the Conservatory must, when called upon, participate in students' recitals and examinations, unless excused therefrom by their teachers and the Director. The importance of this rule is apparent: progress can be definitely observed and officially stated.

Pupils must refrain from whispering or other disturbing behaviour at concerts, lectures, etc.

Pupils are not permitted to take part in concerts outside of the Conservatory without the approval of their teachers.

The presentation of flowers at the students' concerts is not permitted.

Loud conversation, noise and laughter in the corridors are forbidden.

Pupils must examine the notices on the bulletin boards.

Failure to do this results in many misunderstandings and disappointments.

LOUGHEAD & CO: MFRS. PHILA., P